FIGHTING OFF DEPRESSION; Proven Steps To Help You Fight Depression And Live A New Life

Terry S. Williams

Table Of Contents

INTRODUCTION

Daily living may be severely hampered by depression. However, there are several efficient therapies that may help you control your depressive symptoms.

Simple lifestyle adjustments may help you manage these emotions.

There are, however, little measures you can do to give yourself greater control over your life and increase your feeling of wellbeing.

Continue reading to learn how to use these tactics in a manner that makes sense to you.

Chapter 1

DEPRESSION'S IMPLICATION
Knowledge of the facts is helpful in overcoming depression.
Depression may not be "laziness" or a transient reaction to typical loss and/or despair, but rather a medical illness.

Depression Signs and Symptoms

- Moodiness
- Issues with sleep
- A shift in interests (i.e., a lack of curiosity about what you could love) or a lack of drive
- Excessive guilt or an unreasonably poor opinion of oneself

- Alterations in appetite (i.e., eating an excessive amount of or too little)
- Severe anxiety or panic episodes, or agitation
- Suicidal ideas.

Remember that not everyone who is sad attempts suicide. Even if you haven't shown any particular signs of self-harm or suicide conduct, or if your symptoms aren't as severe or chronic as those mentioned above, you may still get treatment.

Adult Depression Warning Signs

Although not everyone is affected by depression in the same manner, the condition is associated with a specific set of signs and symptoms. There is a minimal set of symptoms required for a professional diagnosis of depression, but each person will experience their own unique combination and precise number of symptoms. If you have been dealing with depression for two weeks or more here are the following symptoms:

- Having a constant sense of sadness or depression (or an irritable mood in children and adolescents)
- A decline in interest or enjoyment in once pleasurable activities

- Unexpected weight gain or loss, or a marked change in appetite
- Having trouble sleeping or sleeping too much
- Fatigue or a decrease in energy
- Slowed, agitated, or unsteady actions, words, or ideas
- Feelings of great remorse or worthlessness
- Having trouble focusing, thinking, or making judgments
- Persistent suicidal or death thoughts
- Additionally, you'll display physiological symptoms like fresh, recurring pains or stomach aches. (In certain circumstances, individuals may feel more physically ill than mentally distressed.)
- Attempts to self-treat the underlying mental discomfort might also be indicated by behavioral changes or increasing drug usage.

Male Depression

Although men and women may both experience depression, there are significant disparities in the frequency with which they report certain symptoms.

Men are more likely than women to report the following symptoms of depression:

- Anger\sAggression
- Habit of taking drugs
- Men with depression could also be more prone to engage in some problematic coping strategies, such as workaholism or gambling, reflecting societal norms.
- In addition, males are less likely than women to get a depression diagnosis.

Mood Disorder in Women

In comparison to males, women are diagnosed with depression twice as often. The following symptoms are more prevalent in women with depression:

- Stress
- Indecisiveness
- Anxiety
- feeling pitiful
- Issues with sleep

- Feeling down

Depression in kids and young people
- Anger or irritation, especially about trivial matters
- Loss of interest in previously loved activities
- Irritability
- Extreme shame, blame, or condemnation of oneself
- A weak stomach for rejection
- Social isolation
- Unknown aches and pains in the body
- Angry outbursts or other irrational actions
- Failing to attend class or skipping it
- disagreements with family and friends
- Self-harm
- Suicidal or death-related ideas

Okay, I'm feeling down. Then what?
Simply knowing the signs of depression is not enough; you also need to learn some effective coping mechanisms. Research and drug prescribers, such as psychiatrists, support each

of the following strategies, and these abilities are usually suggested as crucial components of therapy, even for patients who are still taking antidepressants.

Chapter 2

Begin by knowing where you're .

Depression is quite typical. Many individuals are impacted by it, including those in your life. you'll not be aware that others encounter comparable difficulties, feelings, and hurdles.

With depression, a day is unique. It is vital to treat your mental health seriously and acknowledge that you won't always be where you are.

You sometimes need a mild reminder that you are perfect the way you are. "You're enough as you're now," is the message.

Does this contradict your development and transformation objectives and plans? Obviously not. Does this lessen the trauma, sorrow, or affected by your past that you are carrying around with you? Without a doubt. These words enable you to continue pursuing your objectives while meeting yourself where you're with love, acceptance, understanding, and compassion.

Perhaps if we take the time to offer ourselves the compassion and acceptance we need, we'll be better able to strive toward our objectives and keep afloat through whatever challenges or hardships we may have in life.

Chapter 3

Exercise

Give some thought to going for a block stroll. Exercise can appear to be the last thing you'd want to do on days when you don't feel like getting out of bed. However, physical activity and exercise may assist to reduce depressive symptoms and increase vigor.

Your mood could also be significantly improved by engaging in moderate exercise five times each week for 30 minutes each session.

Exercises like yoga, jogging, and aerobics may help boost endorphin production and lessen depressive symptoms. Additionally, you'll exercise without a membership to a gym.

See whether you would be willing to do the opposite of what your mood is asking you to do, like snuggling up in bed, even once you feel like you can't or have very little energy. Set a smaller objective for yourself, like going for a brief stroll around the block.

What fitness regimen makes it a great complement to your depression treatment strategy? There are possibly several variables. Biologically, exercise may stimulate specific chemicals within the brain that can help generate new brain cells and new connections between brain cells.

In addition to the direct benefits of exercise on the brain, additional physiological modifications brought on by exercise, like enhanced metabolic and cardiovascular health, also indirectly support brain health.

Exercise is a superb approach to boost self-esteem and self-efficacy psychologically because you can set little objectives like walking or jogging a certain distance or for a specific length of time. Additionally, exercise may improve your interactions with people socially, especially when wiped out in a group environment such as a class or with a friend or partner.

Chapter 4

Evaluate the component pieces rather than the overall.

Recollections might be colored by painful feelings due to depression. You could realize that you're concentrating on issues that are challenging or seen as being ineffective. Negative thoughts might engulf you if you're depressed. People who are coping with a mental health problem may get mired in a cycle of blaming and self-criticism. If your depression persists for too long, you can experience paralysis and lose the ability to take care of yourself. Everything turns into a reflection of sadness.

Stop trying to generalize too much. Strive to focus on the positive. If it helps, make a list of the significant aspects of the occasion or day. You may keep track of your day's accomplishments and determine which activities you enjoyed.

You may be able to shift your focus to the specific parts that were useful by realizing how much weight you're putting on one item rather than the total.

Chapter 5

Act in opposition to what your "depression voice" advises.

Your inner voice will discourage you from seeking self-help. You can learn to overcome it, however, if you can learn to identify it.

You think the voice is your own and that it is telling the truth about everything. It makes no difference how brilliant or accomplished you are. The real expert on you is your inner super critic. The world could be deceived, but you are aware of your own self.

It just takes one dish to fall to the floor for you to realize how unable you are, how difficult it is for you to accomplish anything well, and what a pointless existence you are living.

You can tell right away whether a coworker is casting you a scornful look by the look on their

face. You are aware that every error serves to
confirm the truth about you, thus you are unable
to forget any error. Because it was an accident
and doesn't count, you are unable to recall any
successes you have had.

You learn to consider different potential readings
rather than jumping to the general conclusion
that you are useless because someone sees you
in a specific manner. When a coworker frowns,
it may indicate that they are angry about
something unrelated to you. You need to
examine things more carefully and question your
judgment.

What were the particulars of the circumstance?
Were you acting in any way to elicit a reaction?
Even if you were, does it always imply that you
did anything wrong and that you would never be
able to do anything right?

But it's unlikely that changing the words in your
thoughts would be sufficient to dispel the notion
that you aren't very valuable. It also wouldn't

totally cure depression. Even though you may be aware that your way of thinking is illogical, you continue to live your life in accordance with it.

Say to yourself, "You could be correct, but it'll be better than simply sitting here another night," when you are unsure if an activity will be enjoyable or worthwhile. You could realize quickly that the instinctive idea isn't always useful.

Chapter 6

Establish a routine
If your daily schedule is disrupted by depressed symptoms, creating a mild regimen may give you a sense of control. These schedules don't have to cover the whole day.

It may be essential to recovery to have a regular structure and routine in your life. Motivating yourself is one factor in this.

People with anxiety and depression sometimes struggle to find motivation. This often results in a deadly loop. You can be sitting there thinking and worried while accomplishing nothing. Then, when you believe you have done nothing, you start to feel even worse about yourself and start to feel frustrated, worthless, and depressed.

For those who are recovering from mental illness, having some framework in place to assist arrange their day is essential. Because regularity and habit don't need a lot of decision-making, they make life simpler. This lessens the very real weariness of always having to make decisions.

Like a workout regimen, developing habits aids in your progress toward a goal. If you do it every morning, it will become second nature. Routines help you regain your motivation over time.

Basic self-care activities like consuming wholesome foods are some of the fundamental components you should include into your routine. But it's also essential to add some diversity to your life. Another choice to think about is a duty, like looking after a pet or watering the lawn.

Take it easy, and don't be too harsh on yourself if you can't keep up with your depression-fighting daily regimen. Try to relax on your terms and give yourself some time. Keep in mind that you may always get therapy and expert support. Put your attention on relaxing and taking care of yourself. That is what fuels us.

Concentrate on developing a flexible but disciplined routine that will enable you to maintain your daily pace.

Chapter 7

Invest more time with your loved ones.
These impulses could be lessened through
face-to-face contact. While you're depressed,
you could stop talking to the people you love
and need.

Converse often with those who motivate you
(not people that bring you down). While it's OK
for you to spend some time alone, try to
maintain a balance and avoid isolation to stop
the sadness from becoming worse.

If you can't physically spend time together, calls
or video chats could be helpful.

Remember that they really care about you.
Avoid giving in to the need to feel overwhelmed.

Chapter 8

Keep a journal or a notepad to record your ideas. Consider journaling or writing about your emotions. Write about your feelings when you're down.
Journaling is a beneficial additional method for tackling mental health issues.

When you put your thoughts on paper, it could be simpler to communicate your emotions. Making a list of your regular symptoms and figuring out their reasons could be helpful.

Everyone needs a way to communicate their intense emotions, therefore keeping a notebook may be beneficial. Although not all studies have reached the same conclusion, some have indicated that expressive writing, which is just putting your thoughts and feelings on paper, may be helpful for those with severe mental disorders.

You may do this simple task however, whenever, and anywhere you please. In a diary, there is no right or wrong way to write. Just keep in mind to develop the habit of writing for at least a little while every day on anything you choose.

Try one of these creative writing tasks if you need some assistance getting started:

- What are the top three things you want to tell your spouse, parents, and/or close friends?
- What challenging feelings or situations do you often encounter?
- What are the three things you use everyday that give you the most joy?

You may make the decision to commit to writing for a little while every day or every week. What matters most is that you can write about anything.

Chapter 9

Create something very different and new
The same brain regions are used while doing the same task again.

According to research, doing new activities may boost your overall happiness and fortify your social connections.

Consider picking up a new pastime, enrolling in a creative class, or honing your culinary skills to take advantage of these advantages.

Choose objectives that you can achieve and that will make you feel successful.
When discussing their goals, most individuals feel awful about how improbable or unreal they are.
A target is reachable if:

- Anything within your control that is
  simple for you (i.e., not too challenging)
  and that you find acceptable (not for
  someone else)
- Measurable (i.e., you know whether it is
  done or not

Instead of thinking, "This is why I'm terrible,"
when anything goes wrong with your goal, ask,
"What can I learn from this?" Use caution when
comparing your progress rate to that of others.
We often contrast our worst flaw with someone
else's best attribute. It's unjust (and usually
wrong)

Chapter 10

Volunteering
You can accomplish two goals at once and spend time with others while learning something new by volunteering and giving your time to someone or something else.

Look for small chances to assist others. Become personally fulfilled by making a contribution to a cause that is bigger than you. Remember that a service doesn't have to be vast to be valuable.

Even though you might be accustomed to receiving assistance from friends, reaching out and providing assistance may improve your mental health more.

Studies have shown that while many of us have a propensity to focus on our own needs, doing so may actually lessen the symptoms of sadness.

It's possible that by doing so, we are reminded that we are not alone and are given a sense of purpose that we might not otherwise have if we were only considering ourselves.

Anyhow, attempting to make someone else's day better is never a bad thing. Kindness and compassion don't have to be expensive or time-consuming. Simple deeds like taking a cup of coffee to a friend who may be in need or holding the door wide for someone who looks to be carrying a lot might make a significant impact.

Volunteers also reap physical benefits. One of these advantages is lowered risk of developing hypertension.

Chapter 11

Work on your diet.
There isn't a miracle meal that will make you happy again. What you put into your body, however, may really and dramatically affect how you feel.Concentrate on how the foods and beverages you are consuming affect your mood.

Eliminating sugar, preservatives, and processed foods may also improve some people's energy levels and general well-being.

Are you aware that eating processed foods may increase your risk of depression? While it's normal to eat them sometimes, it's not a smart idea to make an unhealthy diet a part of your regular routine. Your dietary consumption must be documented.
Your breakfast should include fresh fruit, your lunch should include protein, and your supper should include veggies.

Including lean meats, vegetables, and grains in your diet might be a great place to start. Reduce your intake of alcohol and stimulants including caffeine, coffee, and soda.

To discuss the ideal dosage and any potential risks, it is advisable to first speak with a healthcare professional if you're interested in taking specific supplements for your depression. Some supplements could be dangerous or interact poorly with any medications you might be taking if you take them in excess. Your doctor might order a blood test to see if you are nutrient deficient before prescribing a supplement.

Chapter 12

Work on lowering your alcohol and drug intake. Alcohol and drugs are two substances that may make depressive symptoms last longer.

On the other hand, those who battle addiction could exhibit depressed symptoms.

Reduce or stop using alcohol and other drugs if you want to get rid of the symptoms of depression.

When someone is depressed, substance abuse is common. You might be more prone to using alcohol, marijuana, or other drugs to treat the symptoms of your depression. It's unclear whether using drugs and alcohol makes depression worse. But continued drug use can alter how your brain works, exacerbate pre-existing mental health conditions, or even result in the development of new ones.

Chapter 13

Making Sleep a Priority
It might also have an obvious effect.
Depression frequently causes problems sleeping.
You may have problems falling asleep or
sleeping excessively. Both might make
depression symptoms worse.

Every night, try to get at least 8 hours of sleep.
Make an effort to create a regular sleeping
routine.

Get the right amount of sleep to achieve
equilibrium. Staying up late one night and
sleeping in a lot the next day is a certain way to
foster unhappiness. Don't try problem-solving
late at night when your brain is only partly
awake.

It could be good to go to bed and wake up at the
same time each day if you want to stay to a

pattern. If you get adequate sleep, you could feel more balanced and energized throughout the day.

Chapter 14

 Accept the truth of your emotions.
To manage the difficult depression symptoms, it could seem prudent to compartmentalize and control your emotions. However, this approach eventually fails and causes damage.

We validate ourselves when we recognize and accept that our beliefs, feelings, and motivations make sense.

They may not be cordial. They could not feel as if they fit in. Unease may set in. Nevertheless, they are what they are.

This following actions could help us validate ourselves:

- Identify any strong tendencies you may have.

- Keep in mind that it's OK to think, feel, and have impulses.

- Consider whether you are being sensitive to these feelings or if you are resisting them.

- Try to create good attitudes toward yourself, your thoughts, and feelings over time, such as openness, acceptance, patience, and self-compassion (being deliberately nice to oneself) (being actively kind to yourself).

- If you are feeling passionately and are forced to act in a way that can cause troubles, try to calm yourself, take a deep breath, and make a decision that will aid.

- Recognize if you're having a poor day. Try to focus your attention on engaging in productive tasks rather than concentrating on your emotions when you become aware of and acknowledge them.

For self-healing and holding on to hope, it may be useful to comprehend how depression symptoms come and go.

Chapter 15

Considering medical treatment
It could also be helpful to discuss your situation with a professional. Your primary care physician may be able to suggest a therapist or other professional for you.

They might assess your symptoms and work with you to develop a specialized clinical treatment plan. This might include a variety of options, such medication and therapy.

Be honest with your doctor or another healthcare practitioner about what is and isn't working so they can determine the best course of treatment for you. They'll work with you to decide which option is best.
WARNING: Consult your healthcare professional before abruptly stopping any prescription antidepressants. With your

physician, go through any queries or worries you may have about the negative effects of your prescriptions.

Conclusion

You could feel powerless if you're depressed. You aren't. There are many things you may do on your own to fight back, in addition to treatment and perhaps medicine.

Fighting depression is not an easy process, but if you make up your mind to do it, nothing can stop you from succeeding, and in the end, you will be glad you made the effort.

Never be too proud to ask for assistance since you never know when it could come in handy.

Never give up on yourself because nothing is insurmountable.

www.ingramcontent.com/pod-product-compliance
Lightning Source LLC
Chambersburg PA
CBHW051718250726
48653CB00008B/3088